Thoughts From Afar

Also by Michael P. Maurer

A Journey Through A Warrior's Soul

Thoughts From Afar

A Collection of Poems

by
Michael P Maurer

Perfume River Publications

Copyright © 2007 Michael P. Maurer
All Rights Reserved

ISBN-10: 1-934478-03-2
ISBN-13: 978-1-934478-03-5

The cover photo and all text in this book are the exclusive property of the author. No part of this book may be used or reproduced in any manner whatsoever without written permission except in the case of brief quotations embodied in critical articles or book reviews.

The author may be contacted at mpmaurer@hotmail.com

Perfume River Publications
52 Chamayanusorn Road
Parknum Muang
Krabi 81000 Thailand
perfume.river@hotmail.com

Edited by Robert Bystrom

Printed in the United States of America by Sunray Printing Solutions, St. Cloud, Minnesota

All net proceeds from the sale of this book go to Vietnam Veterans of America (VVA) for their veteran service and advocacy programs.

For
Jennie and Melissa

Our hope is with our children

Contents

Drifting on New Currents

Changes	10
Rebirth	12
South Facing Windows	13
Paths	14
Holding On	15
Viet Nam	17
Mourning	18
New Home	19
Roots	20
Forgiveness	21
Drowning	22
The Girl in the Tree	23

The River's Edge

Brother Bison	25
Coffee Church	26
Traveling	27
The Sharing Cup	30
Rain Drops	31
At Thirty Thousand Feet	32
Aflame	33
Comfort	34
Shared Past	35
The Mountain and the Valley	37
Hue	38
Reunion	39
Irony	40
The Perfume River I	41
The Perfume River II	42
The Perfume River III	43

Gazing at the Moon

River Moon	45
What about Love?	46
Ocean Memories	47
Thoughts of You	48

Respite by the River	49
Her Love	50
Life After You	51
Whispering	53
Early Morning Dreams	54
The Price of Love	55
My Love	57
Together	58
Love's Transitions	59
Stirrings	60
A Quiet Agony	61
Fading	62
Going Slowly	63
Falling	64
Near You	65
Promises	66
The Truth	67

Dark Nights

Deluge	69
Scared Of Myself	70
Alone	71
Self Pity	72
Bleeding Words	73
The Snake Lady	74
Lonely Coffee	76
Despair	77
Drumming	78
War Money	80
Sorry We're Full	81
Atrocities	82
Self Reflection	83
Consequences	84
Suffocating Quiet	85

Listening to the Waves

On Being Men	87

The Past	88
Distant Mountain	89
The Water Buffalo	90
Blurred Reality	91
Next to Our Youth	92
Remembering Veterans Day	93
Voices	94
Angel Fire	95
Places	96
Sky Candles	97
Illusions	98
Fishermen	99
Tireless	100
Digging Boulders	101
Baggage	102
Cutting Words	103
Broken Boats	104
Clinging	105
Crashing Waves	106

Walking Toward the Sun

The Wind	108
Ripples	109
Dancing	110
Beauty	111
Savored Moments	112
Journey's Guide	113
Liberation Day	114
Spirit Voices	115
The Keeper	116
Rocking	117
Comfortable lives	118
Outdoor Theater	119
Returning	120
The Perfume River IV	121
Home	122
Waiting for You	123
One	124

Drifting on New Currents

Changes

I walk upon
A golden path
Of newly fallen aspen leaves.

I move along the inviting carpet
Toward promise of something more,
Not sure where I am going
Or what I will find.

The leaves sing
In continuous, lively melody;
They compress and break under my weight
Sacrificing themselves
To cushion my steps.

The surrounding woods seem endless;
Trees nearly bare,
Silent sentries to my journey.

Sense of any other world,
Any other existence
Given up to them.

They stand proud,
Their glorious garments
Scattered around.

Tall with reaching limbs,
Unashamed even in nakedness,
They bask in unobstructed sun.

A few leaves
Cling to their branches,
Resisting inevitable change,
Crying out as they spin and wave,
Stubborn to the last.

The world changes;
Life changes like the seasons,
But like unyielding leaves
I cling to the past,
To old routines and comforts,
Afraid of change.

Moving forward,
Farther from my beginnings,
From my reference points,
I am drawn by invitation of the trees
To drop my garments.

Slowly with each step,
With each mile,
Still crying out in resistance
Like the clinging leaves,
I let go of clothing
That obstructs the sunlight.

I let go of fear,
My disguises,
My self-deception

Until I stand naked in the sunlight,
Arms stretched wide,
Embracing nakedness,
Inviting and embracing change.

The last leaves fall;
Truth stands all around me
Proclaiming the importance
Of transitions,
Of change.

Rebirth

I curled up
Upon myself
Inviting the darkness,
The quiet.

I curled up
Into a cocoon
Of separation,
From what I was
And what I knew,
That I might see myself
Free from the judgments of others,
Understanding
For the first time
Who and what I really was.

I curled up
Upon myself
Inviting the darkness
Where I found myself.

I curled up
Upon myself
Awakening in a new place,
To a new life,
A new birth.

South Facing Windows

South facing windows
On the second floor;

A promise of sunshine,
Warming,
Illuminating.

New paint,
New views.

Fresh snow
Offers new perspectives,
New landscapes.

First footsteps in the snow;
A path
To new beginnings.

Reconstruction and repair
In the house,
In our lives.

Vacant rooms,
Long held dreams,
Promise of new life,
New joys.

Physical changes;
Spiritual journeys
Warm with memories.

The promise of sunshine
Within and without
From south facing windows
On the second floor.

Paths

Hope rises in golden rays
Above the mountains,
Quickly fading to a pale glow
Across the expanding blue wash.

Hope grows with the light,
Exposing choices,
Offering countless paths.

I walk toward the mountains
And the glow,
Making small adjustments in my course
And thus my destination.

Holding On

I clung tightly,
Holding on to the safety of the rock
In the midst of life's river,
Finding comfort in familiar surroundings.

I knew the importance of rocks
And the safety they offered,
Having nearly drowned
In raging streams before.

Preoccupied with safety,
I clung to the rock,
Knowing its form
And my place in the river.

Experience was limited
To events near the rock
Or things carried by the stream.

Still I was afraid to reach out
To grab them,
Even with one hand,

Afraid that letting go
I would drown,
Or be carried away,
Left to drift helplessly
Without the comfort of a familiar rock.

But currents swelled,
Buffeting my rock,
Loosening my grip.

I found new courage;
Or was I just weary?
Maybe I simply lost the need
To hold onto familiar ground.

Surprising even myself
I let go,
Giving up to the currents
That quickly carried me away,
As others cried out from their rocks
In fear and panic,
As much for themselves as for me.

It must have scared them
To see that they could let go and survive,
That they had a choice
When they told themselves they had none.

The stream carried me in many directions;
At times I was afraid
But more alive than when clinging to the rock.

I experienced new and interesting places,
Found other cultures,
Met new people
Who had let go
And were riding the current as well.

In calm times,
Rocks still offered themselves,
But if I hold on now
It is just to visit;
A short respite
In a continuing journey.

Viet Nam

Her wounds have healed
As have mine.
She welcomes me
And pulls me to her breast.
We forgive each other.

Mourning

Four days,
So little time to say goodbye.
Four days
To leave friends
And possessions that mean nothing next to friends.

A sudden eviction
From a country that was home,
Then and now.

Suspicions become reality in paranoid minds.
Some scars resist healing,
Others torn open by fresh insults on the global stage.

Preparing to depart,
Carrying more sadness than luggage,
Leaving home and friends
For an uncertain destination.

Sadness hangs in the air;
More people than I know are mourning.

A man says, "All of Hue is crying."
Another says, "People are good,
Governments are bad."

We mourn together.
Life is made of loss
And mourning.

This is just one more time;
One more loss
In a stream of times,
A stream of loses.

We must learn to mourn well
To live well.

So I mourn
That I may live.

New Home

The river is familiar
But I've never been here.

I walk along its length
Through the town,
Past shops and gardens.

I pause to catch my breath,
Savoring the fragrance
And the feelings;

Aware of movement
To me and from me.
Another river's gift.

Re emergence,
New beginnings,
The offer of a new home.

I can stop searching,
But not moving;
I can move ahead from here.

Roots

A ripping sound.
New roots torn.
A tree pulled from the ground
To be replanted.
One of countless relocations.

Moving to new sites,
Torn from old,
Compelled by forces
Hard to understand.

Settling in new ground.
Roots form
To be pulled again;
Tearing hair roots
Freshly grown.

A ripping sound.
Piercing pain.
Countless nerve endings torn.
Screaming!

Moving to another place.
Lingering just enough
To start new roots;

Then move again.
Unable to stay,
Compelled by forces
Without understanding.

A ripping sound.
Heart felt pain.
New roots tearing.
Hidden tears.

Pain
Reaffirming life.

Forgiveness

Each smile,
Handshake,
And bow,
Every cup of tea offered,
An act of acceptance and forgiveness.
If you can forgive me
Shouldn't I be able to forgive myself?

Drowning

I struggle to the surface,
Gasping for breath,
Drowning
In a sea of memories.

The weight of the years
Overwhelm me,
Stealing my breath.

"If only" a life preserver
Floating just out of reach.

The faces,
Alive and dead,
Parade before me.

The regrets,
A millstone
Assuring my fate.

But a brilliant light,
Seen even from the depths,
Keeps me struggling toward the surface,
Reaching for the next breath,
Refusing to drown.

The Girl in the Tree

Sacred ground.
Rows of graves.
Soldiers from another war
Buried near the place they fought and fell.

Imagined lives;
The chaos and horror of battle
Played out again on the same ground
With different armies.

Sadness
Rises from the soil,
As real as the stone markers,
Monuments to the worst of human interaction.

Every step
Brings more graves.
Movement a great effort.
So many graves on so many fields.

Among the graves,
A young girl
Perched in the branches of a tree
Clutches a small, white flower.

Looking,
Without tears,
Motionless,
Holding the flower.

A sea of death,
Garden of stones.
A girl keeping a vigil.
Blossom white with innocence,
The fragrance of hope.

The River's Edge

Brother Bison

The bison are our brothers.
They speak to us
And we to them.
Their spirit is in us.

We follow them across the plains;
The plains of our ancestors
And of their ancestors.

We travel across the same ground
In ebb and flow
Connected by the eternal bond of life.

They offer themselves to us
And we honor their spirit;
They provide us with the instruments
For their offerings.

They feed and clothe us,
Shelter us
As brothers do,
Honoring us,
Sustaining us with their presence.

We worship them,
Their countless numbers,
More numerous than all the tribes.
We thank the Great Spirit for the gift.

We are brothers
Throughout time.

As long as there is a sun,
As long as there is a moon,
We will travel these plains
Together as one family.

Coffee Church

A gathering
On sidewalk stools.

Warm greetings,
Communion in cups,
Shared stories and prayers.

Holding spirits if not hands,
Offering friendship and comfort.

Mornings spent
At coffee church.

Traveling

The city closes in
Or perhaps something is calling,
Something from the past,
From our beginnings.

Driving away,
The direction is less important
Than the image in the rearview mirror.

Leaving the freeway
For quieter roads,
Lower speed limits,
Slower movement.

Escape brings relief;
The excitement of moving towards
Some unnamed destination
Not on any map.

The road climbs,
Rolling hills,
Berms separate one world from another.
The landscape now untamed by machines
That level city roadways.

Interior landscapes change;
Tension fades,
Recognized only by its absence
Like a winter coat shed in spring
Bringing lightness.

Asphalt roads turn to gravel,
Two lanes becoming one.
Cornfields, pastures and cows
The new skyline.
Concrete and towering buildings
Just a memory.

Thoughts of nature
Replace appointments and to-do lists.
New vistas bring serenity.

Meandering streams and winding trails,
Traveled by creatures
Wild and tame,
Replace concrete walkways
That wear out feet and minds.

Corn and cows
Give way to lakes and trees;
Sign posts of transitions.
Closer to that which calls.

Calmness flows,
A rising tide
Washing away the scars of the past,
Creating a matrix for a new day.

The gravel road turns to dirt,
Winding around trees and ponds,
More a cartway than a road.

Life slows;
Each tree,
Each leaf
Visible in clear detail.

Cooler air,
Smells of nature
Beckoning.

Not a place for vehicles;
Immersion only found on foot.

Walking
Without purpose,
Without direction,
Without concern.

Feeling,
Smelling,
Tasting the grass, the flowers, the trees,
The lakes, the streams, the river.

Tall grass caresses,
The trees bow their branches in welcome,

The leaves chatter with excitement,
Soft breeze a gentle guide.

The essence of beginning
Crowding around,
Nudging one another gently,
Offering their embrace,
The city long forgotten.

The Sharing Cup

We pass one cup
Each of us drinking in turn.

The rice wine is clear and strong,
Hot in our throats.

The cup is passed,
Another man speaks then drinks.

As one drinks
We all drink.
We are one body.

There are no tears,
Just the sharing of the wine
From the one cup.

An empty chair
Marks the absence of friends
From long ago,
Of recent days
And of tomorrow.

Each man toasts in turn,
Speaking of memories and friendship,
Marking our present and our pasts.

We share more than wine:
Connections through the years,
Our grief at parting.

We are men,
Some former soldiers,
Some former enemies.
Today we are friends,
Closer because of our pasts.

We pass the cup
Sharing the wine and friendship.

There are no tears.
Only a promise of meeting again
And the sharing cup.

Rain Drops

Soft dance of rain drops.
The city blurred
Like some vague thought
Not quite recalled.

Memories drift in and out,
Stirred by the rhythm
And blurred images.

The breeze stirs,
Carrying wetness;
A soft touch
Like a gentle hand.
A reminder of other tender touches.

The rain continues to dance,
Creating its own melody.

Drifting in and out
Through blurred images
And rain stirred memories.

At Thirty Thousand Feet

Dreaming.
A conversation
At 30,000 feet.

Minds and passions filled
With possibilities.

Dancing slowly,
The verbal dance that people do
Aware of the fragility of new connections.

Snapshots of lives
As the plane raced toward a destination
And a separation.

Dreams unrealized.
Strings from the past.

Weaving a beginning,
Mindful of the end.

The connection
Created by the end.

Opening memories,
Regrets
We could walk away from.

The wheels bounced against the runway.
Things went unsaid.

Different destinations.
Promise and hope hanging in the air.

Aflame

Conversations continued
But the room grew still.
Aware only of her.

Drawn to her
By some power
That I had no hope of controlling,
No hope of understanding,
Nor did I care.

Green pools
Sparkled in the light
Hiding the secrets beneath.

Hair aflame.
A fire that consumed me.
I surrendered to the heat.

She drew me in and pulled me down
Until I fell endlessly
Not caring if I stopped.

A thousand words were passed
Without any being spoken,
Igniting new fires.

She extended her hand,
I held it for a lifetime.

Comfort

We clung to each other
Like to driftwood
In turbulent seas.

It wasn't what we wanted
Or needed,
But it kept us afloat,
Gave us comfort.

We were tossed and thrown
By the waves and currents
Of our lives.

We were alone on the vast ocean,
Clinging,
Waiting
For more sea worthy vessels.

We clung to each other,
Taking comfort for the moment
In the warmth
Of companionship.

Shared Past

I sat by the river in those first days
Drinking thin, powdered coffee
From a small tin can
That was my cup for months.
The residue of past drinks clung to the cup,
A strange scrapbook of travels and meals.

My rifle rested on my lap,
A constant companion
Never far from my grasp.

I watched the river nervously
And the trail that ran beside it,
Never sure of my safety.

I am drawn to the river again and again
As to an old neighborhood where one grew up.
I did grow up beside the river.

We met when I was young,
Too young.
The river was my teacher.
I left when I was old,
Far older
Than the year we passed together.

Returning today to visit
Is like sitting with an old friend;
The river knows things about me that no one else knows.

The river is peaceful now.
There are plastic chairs and small tables.
Coffee is served in clean glasses,
A thick, flavorful blend.

I hold a book rather than a rifle.
My body older,
My senses less keen,
My mind full of memories.

The trail is cobblestone.
Students and lovers stroll along
Too young to share the river's past.

I wonder if they can hear the river's voice,
Understand the stories
Or know her secrets.

The river seems different;
Maybe we are both more peaceful
Or perhaps only I have changed.

I am calm,
The fear is gone,
Left somewhere
Or carried away to the sea
Like other residue of those days.

I listen to the river closely,
Now as then,
But with the wisdom of years
I hear new sounds.

The river is a friend.
One of few remaining from that time.
I see her differently today,
Not as a barrier or a water source
Or something to be fought over.

Some of us died to hold her,
But today no one contests my presence.
Today the river holds and comforts me
As only old friends can.

We share our secrets and memories,
Our dreams for the future,
Both of us moving slowly
On the same course
But with new perspectives of the past.

The Mountain and the Valley

The chanting drifts faintly on the breeze
Like smoke from wood fires.

Climbing forward
While drifting back;
The past and the present joined here
Like the mountain and the valley.

The mountain
With its bunkers collapsed and overgrow,
Only remnants and memories of the past,
The guns and soldiers decades gone.

But the feeling of what happened here
Still hangs in the air;
The residue of violence and suffering
Rise with the dust,
Having seeped into the soil along with the blood,
A permanent part of the landscape.

New residents in the valley
Build temples in the shadows of the past.

Mountain and valley,
Temple and bunkers,
Prayers of different kinds.

The breeze shifts and rises from the valley.
The chanting grows louder,
Settles over the mountain.

Monks offer prayers
To soothe and cleanse
The land and the spirits.

The ghosts of the past
Joined with hope of the future
Like the mountain and the valley.

Hue

The skies over Hue are weeping,
Not with sadness but with joy.

We walk through her streets together,
Through her tears
And add our own.

Reunion

The violinist
Plays passionately,
Caressing the strings with his bow,
His music touching our souls.

Sharing tears
For the joy of the music
And the company of friends.

Holding hands
As the music hold us.
Each note celebrating
Our reunion.

Irony

She holds my hand
Through the streets of Hanoi,
Down the streets of her youth.

She speaks softly,
Smiling at me,
Squeezing my hand.

She says nothing of the time
When we were enemies;

She speaks only of her city,
Her love evident.

I smile back
Lost in the irony
Of the loving union
Of war torn souls.

The Perfume River I

The river whispers
As I sit beside her,
Her voice soft and soothing.

We talk of the past,
Of our time together,
Of the things we gave each other,
Some best forgotten.

We have each gone on since then,
Yet we are together,
Bound by a shared life,
A shared time,
And though different,
We are the same
Unchanged through time.

We hold each others lives,
Flowing forward together
In a bitter sweet reunion.

Perfume River II

We have an intimate past
Few have shared
And fewer will speak of.

You have nourished me
With the sweetness of your waters.

You have bathed me,
Cleansing my body if not my soul,
Washing away the blood
Of enemies and friends.

You have comforted me,
Accepting my tears,
Holding my sorrow.

You have hid me
In the lush growth along your banks,
Keeping me safe
When most went wanting.

You have guided me
Through your valleys
And along your tributaries,
Always bringing me back
To the comfort of your waters.

You have waited patiently
All these years
For me to come home
And talk with you again.

We talk now,
Sharing secrets few will ever know.

Perfume River III

How can I not love you?

You always whisper to me,
Sharing your stories
Of places you've been
And the things you have seen,
Of the mountains and the sea.

How can I not love you?

Each night you capture the colors of the sunset
And make them dance for me.
You hold the moon,
Expanding its radiance
In sweet reflections.

How can I not love you?

You tell me stories of lovers
Who have gathered through the years along your banks.
You tell me of the travelers and goods
You have carried.

How can I not love you?

You share your joys and your sorrows,
You delight in my joys,
You carry away my sorrows
Without questions or judgments.

How can I not love you?

You embrace me
At each visit as though I have never left,
Offering me understanding,
Forgiveness,
Comfort and hope.

How can I not love you?

Gazing at the Moon

River Moon

The moon rises,
The river dances in its radiance.

I wonder if you see the same moon.
I wonder if you are watching the same dance.

I wonder if the moon
And the dancing river
Remind you of me.

What about Love?

"What about love?" She asks.
Not that she was offering.

"I have it," I tell her.
It's just different than she envisions.

"You don't have to be sleeping with someone
To have love,
Sometimes it just complicates things."

"Yeah," She says shaking her head.
"But what about love?"

Ocean Memories

The ocean washes over her,
She bounces in the surf,
Turning her back to each wave,
Surprised when a larger wave catches
And rolls over her.

She disappears momentarily.
There are only the waves
As though she was never there,
As though I had been dreaming.

Then she rises,
Smiling,
Laughing,
Water running off her hair
As if reborn in that moment.

She walks toward me,
The water falling away,
Her wet skin glistening in the sun.

Her smile grows with each step,
Her joy obvious.

Her pink suit clings tightly,
Her nipples large and dark
Visible through wet fabric.

She continues toward me,
Smiling,
Quickening her steps.

Then she is gone.
There is only the ocean,
Only the waves.

Thoughts of You

A fisherman in a small boat
Sets up at dusk near a reed island to try his luck
Like a scene from other places I have known.
I watch the fisherman and the sunset
And think of you.

Conversations from tables around me
Drift in and out;
The words are foreign,
But I watch the couples talking,
Leaning in to touch each other as they talk
And I think of you.

The lights of the city begin to glow
In the gathering darkness,
Reflected in the river,
But I sit alone in this romantic setting
And think of you.

The traffic soundlessly crosses the bridge.
At times the city seems distant
Even as it holds me in its constant motion.
I watch the traffic come and go
And think of you.

Sometimes things seem so bright and clear
Like the lights of the city.
Other times I am confused,
Things are blurred
Like the reeds drifting in and out of focus
Just below the surface of the river.

Your love was like that.
I watch the lights
And the reeds
And think of you.

Respite by the River

The great river flowed beside us
With all its stories and its past,
But only her stories interested me.

She held my attention as she held my heart;
She bared her soul
And opened her heart to me.

The beauty of the river surrounded us,
But her beauty held me
And I gave myself to her.

She allowed me to touch her
As she had touched me
And I held her beauty in my hands
And caressed it.

The great river continued to flow,
But time stopped.

I rested in her presence,
An hour or a week,
Gaining strength to continue the journey.

Her Love

Her hand
Reaches for mine,
Closing the distance.

Her fingers touch my hand,
My body tingles,
My heart sings.

She pulls me tightly beside her.
Safe and warm,
I feel her love.

Life After You

I thought I was okay,
That my life was okay,
Full,
If not rich,
But you changed that.

Life is not the same.
How could it ever be?

Everything pales next to that time.
I judge new friends by you,
But who can measure up?

I wasn't lonely
Until you came into my life,
Opened my heart,
Then left.

Perhaps it is why we met.
Do you believe in such things?

Cultures and miles separate us,
Two generations always did,
But more important things connected us.

You took me to new worlds,
Foreign places and new feelings.
You showed me a kind of friendship
I'd never known
Or had long forgotten.

You trusted me with your life,
Gave it all so freely
Without reservation or cost.

You teased me,
Laughing at my silliness,
The games with the children,
Sock rides across classroom floors.

You laugh at the adults
Who seeing me with the children
Believed I spoke the language,
When you knew better.

There was an easiness,
A comfort between us
Of long held friendships.

You listened with interest and intensity,
Delighting in your knowledge of me,
Knowing yourself to be the sole keeper.

You loved me in your own way,
Different than I had known,
And I loved you.
Though it always went unsaid between us,
We both knew.

I was alive with you,
But I sensed you'd been alive for ages.

You taught me so many things,
Mostly how to be alive,
Exposing my safety and emptiness.

But the most difficult lesson
You are teaching me by your absence:
To remake my life
And learn to live without you.

Perhaps that was always the point,
The real lesson you were sent to teach me.

I live new days,
Always aware of your presence
And the things you taught me.

Whispering

Honey brown beauty,
Full lips
Spread easily into an uncertain smile.

Frightened of herself,
And of him.

Wanting,
But not wanting.
Being careful,
Trying to be safe.

She whispers a word,
Tentatively,
Wondering if he'll respond.

She waits anxiously
For the soft touch of his breath,
Reassuring words,
Whispers of new lovers.

Early Morning Dream

A drink of cool sweetness
That barely touched my lips.
A soft melody left unfinished.

Awareness.
Warm breath, racing hearts.
Then nothing.

Searching clouded memories
Trying to recover the image.

My tongue lingers on my lips,
Hoping for some evidence of the sweetness
To help recall the moment.

Thirsty for another drink,
A longer moment,
Hoping to taste the sweetness again,
Hold it in my mouth,
Savoring all that it is.

Hungering for the melody,
The voice that sang to me,
That teased me with thoughts too fragile to hold.

Moving slowly through the fog,
Looking for something solid,
Some residue of love
To know that it was real
And not a dream.

The Price of Love

The room was warm and welcoming,
Soft music played
Setting the mood,
Stroking our passions.

A candle flickered on the small table next to the bed,
Its shadow dancing around us
Celebrating the moment;
Its flowery fragrance inviting
As though we lie together under the blossoms of spring.

I lay there in my nakedness
While she touched me,
Tentatively at first
Then with more directness,
More passion.

My feelings soared with the music
She played on my flesh with her fingers.
Her hands were strong and experienced.

Our hands touched,
Our fingers intertwined.
Electricity sparked between us
Casting new shadows on the wall,
New images in my mind.

I moaned in pleasure.
She laughed,
Pleased with herself and the pleasure she gave,
Delighting in her power.

I cared for nothing but her presence,
I prayed for the moment to last.

I imagined lying beside her afterwards for hours,
Listening to her talk,
Savoring the jewels of her stories,
Saving them in a special place
That I might revisit them,

Take them out and hold them
And warm myself in their glow.

I imagined lying beside her,
Watching the fullness of her lips create each word,
Sharing her sorrows
And her passions.

I imagined holding her,
My body alive with her touch,
Each of us comfortable in our closeness,
Feeling safe in each others arms,
Sharing love without fear of rejection or judgment.

I thought of lying there with her for days,
For the rest of my life.

Then her words broke the moment,
The visions crashed around us
And lay shattered on the floor.

She said she was sorry,
But my time was up.

Her words ended the dream,
Pulled the plug on the projector,
The images went dark.

Reality flooded over me
Like a rising pool of dark water
I was powerless to stop.

I dress slowly in the empty room,
Breathing deeply
Trying to scent her fragrance,
To grasp some fragment of the shattered image.

I stepped out on to a dark, empty street
Unsure of what direction to go,
Counting my dollars,
Figuring when I would see her again.

My Love

Her smile
Brings the sun into my days
Again and again.
It warms me with its glow.
The kindness of her spirit
Lights my love.
I am alive beside her.

Together

We were lost,
Suffering,
Damaged vessels
Struggling to stay afloat in the rough seas of life
When we found each other.

We tied our rafts together
And helped each other bail.
We gave one another encouragement and hope,
Spiritual nourishment
And new strength.

We found a great love together
And calmer seas to travel
So we committed ourselves to each other
And built a new vessel to share.

We will journey together,
Enjoying calm seas and light winds.
Holding hands,
We will smile at the beauty of each sunrise.

In rough seas, we will hold each other tightly,
Sharing support and comfort
Until calm seas return.

We will travel together,
Safe in each other's love.

Love's Transitions

Whispered sweetness,
Promises made,
Soft caresses,
Warm embraces.

Unrealized dreams,
Bitter disappointments,
Collected resentments,
Shouted words.

Ugly threats replace sweet promises.
Then, "Have your attorney talk to mine."
How quickly love turns.

Stirrings

A smile through glass,
Barriers of space and time.

Captivating words.
A mystery sown
Like rice seeds
Lying below the surface reflections.

Emotions loosed,
Memories stirred,
Passions touched and controlled.

A sweet fragrance lingers.
A flame lit.
Let it burn to flare or fade.

"Why?" She asks
Wondering.

Perhaps it was only the warmth
Of the breeze
Off the South China Sea.

A Quiet Agony

The days drag by,
A quiet agony.

Marking time,
Unable to breathe
As though your absence
Has sucked the air
From the room.

Recalling your face,
Fearful that I might lose the image.
Your eyes look back at me
Pleading,
Searching for understanding.

Your smile fades
As though it has become a
Great effort to smile.

Are you struggling too?

The connection is scratchy.
"Fine,"
You say,
But your voice
Lacks conviction.

Are you suffering
Your own quiet agony?

We count the days
Till our reunion,
Both scared
It might not come.

Lacking strength
To reassure one another,
We mark time,
Struggle to breathe
And watch the calendar.

Fading

Some things fade
Like the light of day,
Dropping away
Towards darkness,
Imperceptibly
Until all there is darkness
As though that is all there ever was.

So too was love lost,
In bits,
Fading away unnoticed
Until it was dark
And there was no flicker
Or hint of what had existed
Only moments before.

Going Slowly

Go slowly we agreed,
But there was little hope of that.
Like water cascading
Over steep falls,
We tumbled down
Unable to slow ourselves
Until in the deepest pool
The water calmed.
There we clung to one another
Trying to catch our breath,
Keeping each other afloat,
We drifted lazily
Into unknown stretches.

Falling

Your smile drew me,
Your laugh held me.

I watched your eyes dance
To the music of your words.

We walked along the river
Gazing at the flowers and the water.

I watched you move
Elegantly as if dancing,
A sole ballerina,
You held the stage.

I held my breath
Waiting for your answer;
It showed first in your eyes
And offered everything.

Your laughter spilled over me
And I loved you.

The river witnessed that moment
And our promises.

You smiled
And your eyes danced.

Near You

Drawn
As though pulled towards a flame
Without choice or reason.
Lost to any direction but one.
A single purpose,
All else fading,
Only the need to be near you.

Promises

It is different this time,
A planned departure
Not a forced eviction
By authorities that care nothing for love.
We say goodbye easily
With hope of reunion in the air,
Promise in our eyes.

The Truth

Dark Shadows
Clouds across the face of the moon
Illumination
Reflections on the water
Your face caught in the glow
The truth.

Dark Nights

Deluge

A deluge,
Pouring rain.
Memories come like rain
In a sudden downpour.

Rainfall
Broken by green leaves.
Shelter an illusion,
There is no safety under trees.

The raindrops,
Held by the leaves,
Fall long after the storm has passed,
Crashing to earth,
A constant series of explosions
Like the memories
Exploding against the walls of my mind.

Scared of Myself

I have to be careful,
Move cautiously,
Ambushes are hard to detect,
Harder to survive.

Reality and illusion intertwine,
The next attack moments away,
Quick reactions key to survival.

Always alert for the signs,
Flinching even in their absence;
Perhaps I have survived
Too many ambushes.

Danger is everywhere,
Real or imagined
Feeling the same.

I have to be careful,
Nothing is sure,
Nowhere safe.

Reality and illusion intertwine,
A confusing maze
I can't untangle.

Charging ambushes
Seen only by me,
More scared of myself
Than past enemies.

Alone

We are born alone,
Perhaps lonely.

Our mothers hold us to their breasts,
But the comfort is temporary.

We go to school the first time frightened
And alone,
Clutching our school bag
Like a life preserver.

We seek the comfort of friends
Like salve for a wound,
Hanging out in hallways and playgrounds,
Then burger joints and parking lots.

Hiding our aloneness,
Groping for acceptance,
For inclusion.

Boys chase little girls with crawling critters,
Then older girls with groping hands
And yearnings of flesh if not of the heart.

We are blind and alone,
Playing at being together.
We hold on to each other
Carried ahead by whirlwinds of events.

We laugh and cry,
Clinging to one another
In some pretense of not being alone.

But the journey is solitary,
The connections temporary and incomplete.
We stand
Or move ahead
Alone.

Self Pity

Self pity is an unattractive end,
But at times
I fall into the pool
And wallow in it,
Floundering
Until I regain my bearings,
Climbing out
I celebrate my situation
And my choices.

Bleeding Words

The words bleed from me
In a steady flow
Covering the pages,
Pooling around me.

The words bleed from me,
Streaming from my wounds,
Cleansing the abscesses,
Offering hope of healing.

I watch the growing pool,
Fearing that the bleeding might end.

The Snake Lady

She came to me
Offering her beauty
And the warm sweetness of her flesh.

She drew me in,
Disarmed me;
I laid down my weapons
And held her breasts,
Captured in her spell,
Loss in the respite
From the battle.

I sought her mouth,
Her wetness,
But she only hissed,
Her beauty distorting.

She rose up,
Curling around me,
Smiling at her wickedness
And her deceit.

She coiled more tightly
Stealing my breath,
Leaving no hope of escape.

Her head bobbed above me,
Evil shined in her eyes,
She flicked her tongue
To tease me or test the air.

She lowered her head slowly
As though offering a kiss,
Her eyes, dark beads,
Staring without emotion.

She opened her mouth,
Dislocating her jaw,
A gaping black cavern
Closed over me.

She swallowed me
In slow gulps,
Pushing or pulling me deeper
Into the darkness,
Enjoying my suffering.

Life drained from me,
My body went limp;
There was only darkness.

Her tongue darted out
As though to lick her lips,
She seemed to smile,
Her eyes emotionless,
Her belly full.

Rising,
She regained her womanly form,
Reclaimed her beauty,
Walked away
Seeking her next victim.

Lonely Coffee

Sad characters drift in and out,
Sitting alone,
Drinking their coffee.

The same faces
Week after week,
Year after year.

Trying to survive,
Hoping for more.

Hoping for human contact,
For conversation,
For a friend,
Not knowing where
Or how to find them.

Alone,
Lonely,
Drawing some comfort
From the presence of others,
From the din of conversation around them.

Drinking their coffee,
A solitary comfort,
Wishing they weren't alone.

Despair

Where is hope?
Lying scattered on the ground
Like so many pieces of torn paper.

Bits of hope
Blow away,
Scattered in the wind.

Darkness
Is a final welcomed comfort.

Drumming

Drums of war echo across the land,
Beat by old men
Who have never seen the blood of battle,
Who avoided past wars
Through influence and affluence,
Assuring their safety
And political ambitions.

The drumming serves its purpose;
We move toward it
Drawn by the rhythms
And the gathering crowd.

The drumming grows louder,
Ever present
With more drummers
Who fear the label
Of being opposed to the music.

We join the dance,
Moving our feet to the beat of the drums,
Believing it offers vengeance
To cloak our vulnerability.

But those who have killed
In vengeance,
Driven by other drummers,
Know there is no end,
No comfort to be gained,
Only the corruption of the soul.

But most have never learned this,
Trusting surrogates to do their killing.

So we run to the sound of the drums,
Drawn to their seductive beat,
Repeating the chant
Like students of rote learning
Anxious to please the teacher,
Unaware of the meaning of the words
Or of the truth,
Or not caring.

We join our voices with the crowd's
As in the past,
Yelling for violence
From the safety and anonymity of masses.

We rally to the drums
Repeating the selective judgments,
Ignoring the hypocrisy,
Blindly arrogant
In the comfort of our numbers
And our strength.

Part of the crowd,
Lost in anonymity,
We deny our part,
Disown the consequences.
Our voices, our questions
Lost along with our courage
In the beat of the drums,
Beaten by those who gain the most
And suffer least,
Afraid that if the rhythm stops
The crowd will disperse.

Blood flows,
Innocents die,
But not by our hand we believe,
For we did not beat a drum
Or stand at the front of the mob,
We only danced to be part of the crowd.

Only time can expose the hypocrisy,
The deceit,
The hidden agendas
Bought so easily with others' blood
In places we will never see or know.

We stand with the crowd
Believing we are apart from it,
Denying responsibility
While we listen to the drums
And dance to the rhythm.

War Money

While under funded social programs struggle,
There is always money for war.

War is good business for some;
It brings full employment for soldiers and defense workers.

Industries surge producing war materials;
CEOs count their profits.

There are always enough bullets and bombs;
No battlefield is silent for lack of ammunition.

War's destruction
Boosts the reconstruction business;
Corporate leaders and stockholders count their dollars.

Only mothers count the casualties.

Aid work flourishes,
As does fund raising.

Media rush to examine the scene
Creating their own news,
Seeking more viewers
While expense accounts grow.

And no soldier goes wanting
Until after the war.

Sorry We're Full

The hospitals are full,
Their corridors
Lined with broken bodies.

The orphanages are crowded,
More children
Seek entrance each day.

Children cry,
Doctors offer grim faces.

But no war has been stopped
Because hospitals were full.

Politicians and soldiers
From both sides visit
With gifts and promises.

But no war has been stopped
Because hospitals were full.

Children cry,
Doctors offer grim faces.

Soldiers go on fighting,
Politicians smile for the camera
While more bodies
Crowd hospital corridors.

Atrocities

No war is without atrocities,
Evil unleashed by the passions of battle.

What kind of evil
When parents use children
As weapons on their domestic battlefields?

Children reduced to
Collateral damage in war waging
Like dead villagers
Killed by frustrated soldiers.

An atrocity
Driven by rage
Or desire for revenge
Like all atrocities of war.

Parents blind to the evil of the acts
Pull the trigger again and again,
Mindless of the wounds inflicted.
Battlefield rage.

Children are innocent victims,
Dying slowly,
Questioning silently
As most victims do.

Subtle violence
Where there should be love.
Things distorted,
Twisted
Like bodies on a battlefield.

No press corps investigates,
The atrocity undisclosed,
The damage unreported,
Truth remains hidden.

No war is without atrocities.

Self Reflection

I sit motionless in the darkness
My rifle in my hands,
The claymore trigger in my lap,
Tools of death my only company.

I stare into darkness
Watching for movement,
Any movement;
Listening,
Straining to hear,
To gain the advantage
That I may be the merchant of death
Rather than the dead.

I am alert
Despite the late hour
And hard days;
I search the jungle darkness
Looking for answers,
For clarity,
For warnings.

I search the darkness of memories,
Past months,
Past battles,
Trying to remember
Who I was,
What I was
Before I came here,
Before I did these things.

I am afraid tonight,
More afraid than ever,
Not just of the darkness
Or of the jungle,
But of myself,
Fearing that it is too late,
That I am already lost.

I clutch my weapon more tightly
Searching the darkness
For the slightest advantage
That I might save myself.

Consequences

In the past
There was death;
Part of each day.

Some due to my choices:
The wrong trail,
The right one.

Disaster and tragedy
For one side or the other.
Often both.

Death or survival
Determined by choices
Blindly made.

I was both
Merchant and witness.
A price for each choice
Paid by others more than me.

I move carefully now
If at all,
Afraid of disaster,
Afraid of choices
And the consequences they bring.

Suffocating Quiet

Emptiness,
Suffocating quiet.

There is movement,
A sort of going through the paces,
But there is no life,
No living.

There is just the memory of yesterday
And the promise of a too distant tomorrow.

The memory of emptiness
Of suffocating quiet
That goes on unchanged
In a lonely world.

Listening to the Waves

On Being Men

Women touch and hug one another
Without hesitation or concern;
They hold hands
Or rest their hand on a friend's knee,
Accustomed expressions of support and empathy.

Women value human contact,
They understand the comfort of human touch
Offering it freely.

Men don't touch each other
Or seldom do.
They posture toughness
Sharing football scores, car specs,
Fishing stories and fund reports,
Hands on their papers or their drinks.

Expressions of feelings aren't permitted,
A long-held unwritten rule.
Men stick to facts and figures,
To things they know.

None is willing to break the rule,
To risk his manhood
Or ejection from the group.

They sit together but alone,
Suffering quietly in their isolation,
Knowing they are men.

They can only watch with envy,
Wondering who required this of them,
Who taught them these things,
While they go on trying to be men.

The Past

Hue is changing as is all of Viet Nam,
Some cities faster than others.

The beautiful Ao Dia is disappearing
Replaced by jeans and t-shirts,
Traditional dress relegated to ceremonial wear.

More cars vie for road space
Jostling bicycles and motorbikes
Pushed farther to the road edge.

The cyclo is restricted to fewer places.
It may live on but only as a tourist attraction
As some vestige of the past.

Traffic lights are added
Until the number rivals other cities.

Motors hum from the back of small boats
As paddles lay unused along with muscles
And the quiet of the river is lost to memory.

Aid agencies fund the change
Trying to ease the burdens of daily life.
Hand labor and their products disappear,
Assigned to museums
Designated to store and label the past.

English is spoken everywhere
As youth rush to learn the international language.
You must travel to back streets and villages
To hear the music of the native tongue.

Customs and traditions
Die with grandparents,
But few mourn the loss.

Soon one city will so closely resemble another
You will have to read the city sign
To be certain where you are
And visit the museums to find the culture of the past.

Distant Mountain

You are always there,
Unchanged,
Towering over things,
Starring down at me.

Some days you comfort me;
I have eaten your soil
And shared your view,
I have hung onto life
Curled in your belly.

Other days you haunt me,
Holding the relics of my past,
Reminding me that I have been here before
In a different age
As a different person
That is still part of me.

The Water Buffalo

The water buffalo
Plods tirelessly
Pulling its load.

It looks at me knowingly.
I am a buffalo,
A brother.

We move through life
Sometimes as through the mud,
Accepting our loads,
Pushing ahead
At a slow but constant pace.

There was a time
When we stood face to face
Challenging each other,
Each claiming the trail,
Each blocking the other.

You with your black stare,
Me with my black rifle.
Each of us traveling trails
We didn't want to travel
And carrying loads
We didn't want to carry.

We stared and threatened each other
Until one of us chose a wiser course.

Now we stare at each other
Knowing that we are brothers
Pulling our loads through the mud
Until there are no more loads to pull.

Blurred Reality

A trail
Or a dream
Connecting the present and past.

Valleys and mountains
Merge beauty with terror
Until the images blur,
Existing together,
Reality and memory,
The boundaries unclear.

Winds whisper news of the next valley.
Winds of the future
Becoming winds of the past.

A constant traveler
With a clear memory
Announces arrivals and departures,
Beginnings and ends,
Each the same.

The trail is endless,
So is the dream
Only the method of travel changes.

Next to Our Youth

Next to our youth
But so distant from it.

So many steps,
So many lives,
But was it living?

We stand in each others shadow
Near the shadows of ourselves,
Of what we were,
Of what we are now.

What have we become
During our separation?

How did our time together
Change the course of our journey?

Do we recognize one another,
Or ourselves?

We stand in each others shadow
Near the shadow of ourselves,
Next to our youth.

Remembering Veterans Day

It is a day of remembrance
That most forget,
Except my brothers,
Those who survive,
We remember.

We gather at ceremonies, coffee shops or bars
Reaching out to each other,
Seeking something
That remains elusive.

Or we go off by ourselves
To the woods,
To cemeteries,
Both holding our ghosts.

Each of us remembering,
Unable to forget
Battles long ago
And brothers few remember.

For us the remembering is easy,
It is the forgetting that is hard.

Voices

Some speak with quiet urgency,
Some with desperation.

Others scream
Directing men,
Encouraging them,
Trying to inspire courage
When courage is hard to find.

Some scream for aid or ammunition
When neither can be found.

The voices are foreign,
Different tongues of different armies,
A commingling of sounds,
A booming symphony of voices.

Gunfire and explosions,
The percussion instruments
Framing the voices,
The human drama.

I understand the voices;
I have heard this symphony
At a different time,
In different places.

The languages are universal,
They are easy to understand.
The dramas are always the same,
Only minor variations on the theme.

Dien Bien Phu,
One of countless places
Where there will always be voices
Replaying bloody dramas of the past
For anyone with an ear for such music.

I walk across the ground
Slowly,
Reverently
And listen to the voices.

Angel Fire

The sorrow of a father
Rises from the valley.
White wings reaching to the heavens
Silently beseeching,
Drawing others in,
An endless line.
A father's tears mingle
With the tears of others,
With the pain of a generation.

Places

A mysterious place,
Remnants of a royal past,
Testaments to a time.

A history of war,
Ancient and modern;
Scars persist on stone walls
And in peoples minds.

It was the river and the beauty
That first drew people here
To build homes, fortresses and tombs.

It was the river that drew them
With their swords or their guns;
The beauty of the river
Lost in the battles
For transport and commerce.

It is the river and the beauty
That still draws them here
To speak of love
And of children.

Peaceful days
In the shadows of the past.

Sky Candles

The light burns,
One among hundreds
Carrying our dreams.

Growing distant,
Fading in and out
Like our dreams.

A remembrance or a hope,
Something wished for.

But then the light is gone
As is the hope.

Extinguished by buffeting winds,
Or too distant too see
Or imagine.

Illusions

Lights flash,
Circuits spark.

I press my fingers to my eyes,
But the lights still flash.

A copter is down,
Soldiers dead.

The same war,
Or a different one?
Does it matter?

Conversations
Vaguely familiar,
People I should know.

Flashes,
Images
Changing too quickly to grasp.

Illusions or real?
Does it matter?

Fishermen

Men with wine induced grins
Gathered round a table before noon,
Their ships docked,
Their catch cleaned and sold,
Their wages in their pockets
And burning in their throats.

They celebrate their return,
Their luck,
Men who make their livings
And risk their lives at sea.

They celebrate their lives
Or their escape from it,
If only briefly.

Tomorrow
They will gather their gear
And their courage
And return to the sea.

Tireless

Rhythmic sound
Like a beating heart.

The waves break on the beach,
Climbing,
Falling back
Never able to gain and hold it.

But ever trying,
Climbing,
Falling,
Again and again,
The effort endless,
Tireless.

Rhythmic sound
Like a beating heart.

Digging Boulders

The words flowed
Like a stream powered
By spring rains.

A strong current
Flowing unabated,
Undeterred by any obstacle,
Leaving a residue of words
Like a waterline along its banks.

But the stream has gone dry
As if from a summer drought.
The streambed lies
Dry and dusty,
A residue of boulders
Deposited by past flows.

Pages sit unfinished
Waiting spring rains,
Each word buried in the hardening mud,
Boulders in the streambed.

The effort exhausting,
Prying and heaving
Against the weight,
There is some movement,
Finally a word comes forth.

There is no rain,
No stream of words,
Just a streambed,
The residue of past floods,
Empty pages
And the chore
Of digging boulders.

Baggage

Some push it along in shopping carts
With logos of stores closed long ago,
Wheels clattering across sidewalk cracks,
The cart and pusher showing years of wear.

Others carry it in plastic bags,
Bulging and torn,
Pulling heavily on their arms,
Their shoulders drooping from the load.

Some carry it in boxes,
Sorted and indexed,
Easily accessed at the slightest need.

Others carry it in backpacks,
Straps digging into tired shoulders,
The debris of life tied loosely
To the outside of the pack
Flopping with the rhythm of their gait.

But most carry it invisibly:
In the tension of their posture,
In their guardedness or anger,
In their vacant stare,
In the facade of their smile or cheer.

The wounds of youth,
The pain of loss,
The emotional wounds
Collected on the journey
Carried through life.

Cutting Words

Thrown at each other like knifes,
Intended to hurt and maim.

Slashing through the air,
Verbal blades
Cut deeply
Leaving unseen wounds
That resist healing.

Victims and perpetrators
One and the same.

Despite scars of verbal wars
Or because of them,
We unsheathe our weapons
Creating new victims,
New perpetrators.

Broken Boats

Broken boats
Buried in the sand.

Broken hearts,
Grief flowing like the sea.

Sand castles on the beach,
Children playing in the waves.

Tranquility and beauty,
Before and after.

The dichotomy of nature
And of us.

Building and destroying,
Peace and terror
One breath to the next.

Broken boats,
Lingering evidence
Of the power to destroy.

Shattered lives,
Pools of grief
Hidden in the aftermath.

Children playing in the waves,
Broken boats,
The beauty of the sea.

Clinging

Old men cling to their youth
Seeking handholds in the past.

Unwillingly surrendering
Things taken by age.

Telling stories of their strength
Long departed.

Recalling competitions,
Things and people
Won and lost.

Lamenting adventures
Still unrealized.

Sad admissions
Of what will never be.

Games they remember
But can no longer play.

Declining towards the end
While clinging to the past.

Crashing Waves

Waves
Rolling in,
One after another,
Crashing into each other.

One thought breaking up,
Mixing with another.

There is no stillness,
Only the sounds
Of crashing waves.

Walking Toward the Sun

The Wind

It drops out of the Rockies,
Races across the prairies
Scouring the rocks,
Lifting the soils
From Montana and the Dakotas,
Unbroken until it hits the timberline
That cuts across Minnesota.

I taste the wind,
Feel it on my lips
Just as I tasted your love
And the things you brought me.

There is pleasure and mystery
In the wind
As in your love.

I taste your lips on mine now
Even in your absence,
Just as I can feel the wind
Even on calm days.

Ripples

Adrift
Motionless
Sails without breath

Parched lips
Parched soul
Unquenched thirst

A whisper of movement
Soft ripples

Gentle rains
Sweet breath on my face

The touch of a hand
Softness of caressing fingers
Billowing sails.

Dancing

Stepping,
Stumbling,
Beginning again,
Struggling to find long forgotten rhythms.

Tilting my head
Looking for better reception,
Uncertain how to hear the music anymore.

In the distance
The echo of a memory
Fades in and out.

I flail my arms and swirl
With some growing recollection
Of things lost long ago.

Shedding concern
And self consciousness
Like old skin I have worn too long,
I move wildly
To building rhythms.

Closer
As if drawn by my movement,
Louder,
The music drowns all other sound,
All thought.

Spinning faster,
Arms waving above my head,
There is only music
And movement.

I am free,
Dancing
To the long forgotten music
Of my youth.

Beauty

Wonderful radiance,
The early morning sun
Reflecting off dew
On a sea of grass
In a remote meadow.

A soft breeze
Like the gentlest whisper
Moves the grass,
The light dances,
Colors circle,
The meadow alive with brilliance.

Beauty,
Dances before me,
With me,
There is only beauty.

In an instant
The sun's angle changes,
Or the dew evaporates,
The dancing light disappears,
The meadow falls dark
As if all beauty is gone.

I blink repeatedly,
A man woken too suddenly
From a beautiful dream.

But the meadow is just a meadow,
No longer full of dancing light,
Just a meadow
Like so many I've seen.

I move through the drabness
Looking for beauty again
In another hidden moment,
Some other hidden place.

Savored Moments

I shared her mornings,
Moments too brief
But more than I hoped for.

I lay under her cool waterfall
And drank her in,
Thirsty for each drop.

She shared her life,
Trusting me with secrets,
Leading me through newly opened doors.

I kept no secrets from her,
Savoring the safety
And the strength
Of her presence.

Her spirit inspired me.
I was reborn
Nourished by her love.

I danced in her eyes,
Studied her laugh
And delighted in her smile.

I savored each moment,
Clung to each memory
Knowing that time isn't endless.

Now there are only memories
But the moments remain clear,
And there is the new vision
Discovered in her presence.

Journey's Guide

The journey is difficult,
But you are well equipped.

Search your pack,
You have a compass
And a staff.

Silence the din
That is deafening.
Listen to your voice,
Trust its counsel.

Remove the clutter
That is blinding,
See the paths before you.

Feel
The joy and goodness of your spirit;
Nourish them,
Let them nourish you.

Pause,
Listen,
Look within,
You will find a guide
To ease the burden of your steps.

Liberation Day

We celebrate liberation,
The few of us who remember,
Or who have not grown tired
Of others' impositions.

We celebrate liberation
From one government
While suffering another.

Peaceful, subtle oppression
Replaces more violent forms.

Will we ever be liberated from human follies?
From man-made tragedies?

The cycle continues,
One liberation day replaces another,
New governments with new slogans,
A different kind of oppression.

Where is liberation?
What is there to celebrate?

Perhaps the only liberation
Worth celebrating
Is the liberation of one's mind.

The silent, hidden struggle,
The solitary battle,
Won or lost alone.

True liberation,
A victory
Without designation,
Without celebrations or parades.

A freed spirit
Celebrates liberation every day.

Spirit Voices

The clouds build
Climbing high above the mountains,
Giving notice.

The river runs brown and thick
With stories of distant places.

The mountains stand
In undisputed witness.

Blood of the past,
Red blossoms on trees.

The wind carries voices
But few know the language.

Voices of the past
Mingle with voices of the future.

The stories are told
Even when no one listens.

The Keeper

Who will protect beauty?
Who will teach kindness?

Who will be the keeper?

If all is an illusion, what is the meaning?
What is lost when wealth is the goal?

What of responsibility
For truly precious things?

Who will protect beauty?
Who will teach kindness?

Who will be the keeper?

Rocking

Rocking,
Balancing on a chair's back legs,
Back and forth slowly,
An easy motion.

Smooth music
Like the motion of the chair,
Rocking gently with the beat,
Back and forth slowly.

Strong, hot coffee,
A mug held in two hands,
Warmth of the mug
And the motion of the chair.

A murmur of conversation.
Watching people:
Their faces,
Their gestures.
Imaging their moods and their lives.
They come and go,
Moving in and out,
Ebbing and flowing like the sea.
Rocking gently.

Strong, hot coffee,
Spreading warmth,
Rocking back and forth slowly,
Watching,
Part of the scene,
But separate from it.

Rocking slowly,
Tasting the coffee,
Listening to the music,
Watching the movement,
Thinking about where one should be.

Comfortable Lives

Life in the Valley
Looks too easy,
Too comfortable.

People drink lattes,
Shop in exclusive galleries,
Buy expensive decorations
For expansive homes
In gated communities.

They play golf at exclusive clubs,
Attend social functions and elaborate dinners,
Discuss investments and markets.

Hanging out in the Valley
Looks like a comfortable life,
Perhaps even happy,
But it doesn't seem real
So removed from the rest of the world.

Seeing it
Leaves me empty
And frightened
So I run
Seeking something more common,
Something more real.

Outdoor Theater

Coffee in hand,
A constant elixir,
I pause to watch the show.

Streams of people rush by
Oblivious to the palette in the sky,
The changing light on the water,
Colors stirred by a breeze.

Feet hurry in unbroken rhythms,
Thoughts of time and destinations,
Few pause to contemplate the canvas.

The show continues
Even without an audience.
Colors of gods
Replaced by colors of men
And back again.

Today's performance
As spectacular as any I have seen.

I sit with my coffee
In the theater of lights
Feeling no need to travel,
Believing I am where I should be,
Content with life.

Returning

It seems unfinished,
A lingering question
That begs to be answered
Even if its form is unclear.

Sense or not,
It is compelling to return
To places we try to forget
To see what answers
Can be found,
What new paths discovered.

The Perfume River IV

The river flows in two directions
Connecting me to the past
And carrying me to the future.

Flowing to or from the distant mountains
Which stand like ghosts
On the horizon of the past.

To or from the sea,
The reservoir of life,
Waiting to collect the waters of the earth
And all they carry.

The river like life,
Then and now,
Moving towards and from,
Connected.

Passing calmly
Through this time,
Pausing as though to rest or contemplate the journey.
Part and whole merging,
Indistinguishable in the end
From all water,
All life.

As am I,
Part and whole,
Traveling to my own merging,
The river
Connecting mountains and the sea,
The past and the future.

Home

Wanting
Searching
Looking for the comfort of home
To sit on the porch
Watching the sunset
Feeling at peace

Still searching
The longing grows
Along with sadness
Of not knowing where home is
Or how to find it

Tired of the journey
Discouraged by failure
Growing old on the trail
Already old
Having looked in so many places

It is difficult
Traveling without maps
Or signposts
Without knowledge

Maybe there never was
A place called home

Even sadder
Than to have known and lost it.

Waiting for You

The river grows quiet
And dark.

The moon rises
Shining upon it.

I gaze at the water
Waiting for you.

Morning comes,
The sun rises,
But the darkness remains.

I stand alone by the river
Waiting for you.

One

Coffee on the porch
A new sunrise
Renewing old friendship

Inner warmth
Touches the warmth of the sun
Until everything is one.

Acknowledgements

Many thanks to Robert Bystrom, who offered editing help when I most needed it and who helped me see and say things more clearly. Thanks to Fred and Karen Bengtson for their proof reading and helpful comments. Special thanks to Ernie Boswell without whose counsel and support there would be no poetry. Also thanks to the many other teachers who have passed through my life, some for only a moment, most unaware of the teachings and inspirations they offered me. Thanks to family and friends who valued and promoted my first effort and who have encouraged me to complete another. Finally a special thanks to those who inspired specific poems. I hope I have honored their stories.